In the Valley of SPRING LAVENDERS

Somya Sharma

INDIA • SINGAPORE • MALAYSIA

ISBN

Hardcase 979-8-89519-516-1
Paperback 979-8-89475-359-1

For Rahmya

Together and free until eternity

'Goodbyes are only for those who love with their eyes. Because for those who love with heart and soul there is no such thing as separation.'

– RUMI

Contents

DILKASHI

When we first met in school,
In the dining room,
You caught my attention.
I heard your voice, delightfully familiar,
Extending your hand, a gentle 'Hi!'.
I knew it was not love at first sight.

A strange curiosity tickled me,
I kept on wondering,
Why does the voice sound just like mine?

The touch of hands,
The ecstasy of the first meeting,
Like a lost friend, calling me home.
You looked at me,
A feeling so intense, yet familiar.

Who really are you?
Have I ever met you before?

In the lake city,
An alley in which I walked,
Directing me right towards you.

Little did I know,
The next decade,
A journey with you.

Never have I waited for someone,
A moment so true,
You,
Finally, here,
A path anew.
When you walked into my life,
I never knew it was you.

All the time when we ran into each other,
It was a surprise,
An adventure, a gift of a new leaf, a new flower.
A story I never thought would be all mine.

Destiny and fate, playing hide and seek.
Right there, in the midst of chaos,
I felt, for us,
The universe had a plan.

In the Valley of Spring Lavenders

Your eyes—they sparkle like diamonds in the night,
A treasure trove of emotions so sweet, a heart so bright.
I'm drawn to your gaze, like a moth to a flame,
My heart beats fast, for something that's not tamed.

A gleam in your eyes, so bright,
A beam that shines like a warm, golden light.
The child in me wondering, with a curious mind,
Does he know the divine radiance in his own eyes?

A light so bright, shining like the sun, and gold,
Hidden like a story, yet to be told.
I'm eager without fear,
To unravel the secrets and banish tears.

Your voice, a river of melody,
Echoes of sweet harmony,
Comforting and cool, like the shade of a beautiful tree.

The day you called out my name,
Like a soft breeze, flowing around,
Lush green trees, they all proclaim,
Your voice, a symphony so profound.

You are someone from another life,
I've known,
I knew at once you were my only home,
Safe and sound to be around.

I found a place to reside.
A shelter from life's turbulent tide.

Your smile, so sweet.
It lights up the night.
Like a ray of sunshine,
It chases away the fright.

With laughter and giggles, it fills the air.
A joyful melody, beyond compare.

A sound so joyful, it echoes so free.
Like a chime of bells, its music so dear.
A symphony of happiness and of cheer,
A treasure to behold, beyond all fear.

The moon is high, the night is still,
My phone is on, a gentle thrill,
It is you on the line, and I know,
you have a day's tale to tell,
With every beep, my heart does a happy swirl.

My cellphone, now my constant friend,
In the dead of night, our bond deepened,
The silent words, they whispered low,
Of secrets shared, and stories to know.

Always after the whispers,
The silent words made all the sense,
The world outside, a distant pretense,
The night air whispers, a gentle breeze,
As I lay awake, with thoughts that freeze.

Season of spring,
The sparrow chirping.
We stayed up past midnight,
lost in the conversation's stream,
The secrets we shared, like whispers in a dream,
Life's narrative unwinding, like a thread so serene,
As we navigated the labyrinths of our minds.

The never-ending talk, a dance of words so free,
A tapestry of emotions, woven with glee,
The laughter and tears, the highs and lows we see,
A journey of self-discovery,
For you and me.

The morning after, the sun so high and bright,
I survey the world with eager eyes,
Seeking the only one who makes my heart leap.

In the assembly, we're all the same,
But I'm searching for a special name,
For the one that makes my heart dance and throb.

I wait and wait, and then I see,
Your eyes are already fixed on me,
A gentle gaze,
And I know, at that moment, I'm in a daze.

The chats we share, the stories we exchange,
The laughter, making our hearts dance,
The distance between us shrinks,
As this feeling grows, we are closer to our reality.

 In the Valley of Spring Lavenders

Our conversations, like a symphony so grand,
The blood flowing in our veins, my hand is in yours,
yours in mine.
We find ourselves in each other, like a mirror so clear,
And in each other's eyes, we find someone so dear.

The dawn is us; the dusk is us.
We are not like others whom we've met.

'Who are you?' you ask, and when you do,
I see a yellow flame dance in your gaze.

You're more than just a familiar stranger.
And in that moment, the world around us falls silent.
As if, it is our step ahead,
to find the truth buried deep within our soul,
A puzzle waiting to be solved.

Wondering, is Love already playing a role?

With time, nearing the summer break,
My heart begins to beat for you,
Sparks fly high, like stars burning bright.

Our words so short, but full of meaning,
The silence between us, a sweet refrain,
Your face covered, but not your glow,
And I knew then that my heart was yours to hold.

It is going to be the last day before the break.
Another month to go, and I worry with
All the thoughts and just then,

You passed by, with your curious gaze,
searching for me, I feel.
My lonesome heart smiling for the millionth time,
And the whispering wind, singing in my ears,
'He's going to be yours in the coming years.'

In the Valley of Spring Lavenders

UNS

In the month of May, when time was still young,
A week passed by, and I didn't hear from you,
Patience wore thin, like a frail, worn shoe.

The days were long, the nights were dark,
I waited for a sign, a glimmer of your spark.
Like a mirage on a desert's vast expanse,
You vanished, leaving me with no trace or glance.

My mind raced with thoughts, my soul felt adrift,
I questioned my worth.
Was this just a fleeting dream, a brief, sweet thought?
Or the seed we planted then, is now stuck in a drought?

I sat in silence, my heart ached,
Eight days had passed, and my mind wandered,
In a sea of worry, where my thoughts strayed,
And anxiety gripped the day.

My phone rang, a sudden surprise,
A strange number, a familiar guise,
The voice on the other end was one I'd known,
A deep sigh of relief, as my heart moaned.

'Hey', said you, with a gentle tone,
And my worries slowly started to melt,
My mind became calm, as the words did sink,
And I felt my heart leap, with a sense of hope.

The weight was gone, the burden did cease,
As I realized, my fears released,
And though the wait was long and hard to bear,
I still wondered, 'What is this?'
This feeling so rare,
That has never happened before.

In the Valley of Spring Lavenders

In the thunderstorm's mighty roar,
Raindrops dance upon my windowpane once more,
You and me talking again on the phone.

Where have you been, I was waiting all this while.
Didn't I mean anything or was it all a lie?

The world outside so wild, yet at peace,
I stand still,
With tears sliding down my cheek,
Like the happy rain from the sky,
The thunder booms and lightning flashes bright,
I begin to wonder,
What is happening to me?

'You were out of sight, but never out of mind,
Come to your window, I want to see you,' you replied.

Your words like sweet melody,
My heart throbbed with millions of beats,
As I looked outside, it was you in my favourite white shirt.

Eyes, like the ocean so deep,
Smile, like a work of art, so divine and unique,
The way you walked, with grace and with poise,
Made my heart sing, like a sweet, sweet noise.

It was beyond my sense of dream,
To see you standing there,
But oh! Poor boy, drenched in rain.

I smiled and waved, you smiled back,
Our gazes locked in the mutual stack,
The world around us so lost in time,
As our hearts beat in rhyme.

I knew at that moment, this was different,
For this temptation to meet is not in friends,
But in the flush of passion's fire,
That burns within our soul's deepest bend.

          In the Valley of Spring Lavenders

I closed my eyes, and let the feelings consume me,
The feelings that I'd kept locked away,
The longing, the hope,
This feeling so beyond time, yet so true.
It all poured out, like a river's sway.

I couldn't have fallen more that day.
With my eyes closed, I'd say,
At that moment, I knew the truth,
That there's more to this precious youth.

In haste, I ended our call,
And down the stairs, I ran,
My heart racing fast.

In the backyard, I found you,
Drenched, yet standing tall and true,
Eyes twinkling like a star afar.
A smile shone through.

The rain, pelting down,
The sky so aflame with hues,
The air so filled with laughter,
Our hearts full of blues.
We chased each other,
Our footsteps echoed loud,
Our joy and laughter, music, proud and aloud.

We danced beneath the drops,
To the songs of our own delight,
The world around us seized,
And all that mattered was you.

In your arms, I found my home, my rest,
We are One, just seen as two.

    In the Valley of Spring Lavenders

Your finger entwined,
Slowly with mine,
The touch of our hands, a gentle caress.

A feeling so pure and strong yet unknown,
Our hearts beating as one, you see,
In this moment, we are birds of love,
Happy and free.

When we hugged, the stars aligned,
A celestial dance on rhythm divine.
At that moment, the world was blind,
To the magic that we left behind.

My heart, so full of you,
Something in me started to cure.
Is this Love, so true and pure?
A bond that will forever shine through.

We're no longer the same boy and girl we left behind.
A memory of togetherness intertwined,
A moment we'll always find.

After the rain, a lot more of you,
An unplanned date,
A day to cherish.

'You know the way to my heart,' said you.
In a fraction, a moment in time, you said the words loud
and clear,
My mind so amazed, wondering,
My silence and the unspoken words too, he can hear.

Smiles, blushes and a deep sigh,
You drew nearer, me on cloud nine!

I never had an infatuation with the mirror.
My heart yearned for you, differently.
I longed for your gaze that would caress my face,
And in the depths, love that's in its place.

Over the night, in my dreams,
I am reminded of
You and Me,
We were born to untangle the karmic tie.

Born to love again,
Like we have in the past,
Perfecting the art of being together.

Yet still,
Unfolding each knot,
It comes so naturally,
Just like it is, in divine time.

MOHABBAT

What else can be more elegant than two young hearts,
Dreaming of building a home of their own,
High in the clouds, where the air is light,
And where the wind whispers, with all her might.

In this dream, they'll find their peace,
A place where their soul will be free,
From the world below, with its strife,
And find solace in this endless life.

Daily conversations, frequent meetups.
An aromatic sweet delight,
Together we explore nature's delights.

You are my fragrance of peace,
And a flame that burns.
Why am I so much in love with you,
More times in a day than my heartbeats?

In the Valley of Spring Lavenders

Silent hours, late morning showers.
Night walks so late,
Secrets and life talks,
Handwritten letters exchanged,
An urge—what next to set sail?

I spend the evening in a cool shade,
A monument of memories that we've made.

We—
A journey of love that's about to start,
The beginning of building a temple
Of hearts.

I have lately started dreaming and envisioning,
I have loved you in many ways,
Over different eras and in the Milky Ways.

There's a way, we fall back,
Something is still not aligned,
Like we test this course,
Before we collide.

In the Valley of Spring Lavenders

Another day, a bright morning,
You asked,
'I can't stop this feeling. Tell me, where have you been?'

And I thought of all the roads not taken,
My insecurities and dark corners,
Fearing a heartbreak yet all the wait,

I said,
'I was in search,
finding my way to your heart.'

August 1, My Birthday

You gave me a ring that you wore,
With my name engraved on it,
I wear it as a pendant. I still do.

You write me a letter—and ask for a date.

'I love you not only for what you are,
But for what I become when I am with you.
I love you not only for what you have made yourself,
But for what you are making of me.
I love you for the part of me that you bring out,
Can you accept a little of me?'

Something changed that day.
In You,
And Me.

     In the Valley of Spring Lavenders

Scared of heartbreak,
Vulnerable yet anxious of the past,
Trauma that shakes,
Yet with all the words that I could make
I asked you, 'Are you sure you are in love?'
Or is it going to be over like how each of our past selves
did?

You held my hand, and kissed my forehead,
The air of serenity and calm enveloped us.

You said,
'There's a place, a garden,
Where rainbows and flowers take flight,
Trees so tall, their leaves dance,
In a white light,
Meadows and waterfalls, where wildflowers bloom,
Dust to mix, the sun's golden boom,
Birds on the wing, and another side
Is a bright full moon.'

This garden I had in me, so far traveled alone,
With you, this is now my safe home.

We were sure it was the love of a lifetime,
A thousand times in a day,
We were falling deep in love,
A little more today than the previous day.

Until now,
I was looking for someone to grow old with,
But you became my secret to be a child,
Even when old.

Nothing comforted me more than you did,
You are the one unfolding love.

In your arms,
I saw the universe and shooting stars,
And the end of all wars.

You said,
'I am so certain of you,
You can place your trust in me,
And be certain of me too,
And I'd choose you,
Even in my millionth life,
And in a thousand worlds.
This love of ours
Created by the cosmos,
No matter what,
Each time I'd find you,
I'd choose you.
Because it is not the body,
But my soul that loves you.'

A moment of dance in heaven,
The angels twirl and sway with grace,
The beat of drums and the strum of strings,
A heavenly rhapsody of dreams and dreams.
For us, it was all just Love,
Nothing else exists.

You became my promise.
The promise of painting you with my words.
For the rest of my life,
Until my last breath is heard!

AQIDAT

Our love—a flame that burns bright and true,
Amidst the winter's chill, it shines through and through.
Against reason's voice, it dares to speak.
Love that's beyond seasons, and so unique.

The winds of change may howl and moan,
But our love will rise, beyond dusk and dawn.
Through every storm, it will remain,
Love that's strong, and not in vain.

No matter what comes and goes,
Our love will endure and shine.
In the face of adversity, it will stand,
Love that's pure, and in this land.
So let the seasons change,
And the years go by,
Our love will flourish,
And bypass the ocean's deepest tides,
For our love is meant to be,
Even after nothing remains.

Time after Time, in all these years,
Your bright eyes,
And laughter still make my heart leap.

With familiarity
As if we've spent a lifetime,
Like a dancing star that burns bright,
Sights aligned in a way that it triggers,
Our own infinite truth.

You are the dream I wished for, the dream
I had been waiting to wake up to.

And now, awake at last, I see,
That, to me, you're more than just a dream.
You are my reality that will last forever,
My heart that will go on forever and forever.

Together,
All we had was love,
To cherish that, another promise was made,
A promise to sail together in the seven seas.

With our love so strong together,
Even pain will cease.

No matter what,
A promise to sail through every stormy night,
Through every calm, and every shining light.
As many challenges come our way,
We shall face them together, day and night,
Night and day.

In the Valley of Spring Lavenders

Life scrutinizes the promises,
Distance is one such test.
Of lovers' devotion, and love's hidden unrest.

Like threads of gold, their vows do shine,
Yet, the miles between, a chasm design.
The whispers fade, the silence grows,
And doubts creep in, like winter's snows.

School graduation—the walk across the bridge,
And as we stand on the bridge,
The path stretches out.

A different pathway is in sight.
We've crossed many a mile,
Through trials and through strife.

The people we know,
Familiar friends,
Their faces are etched in our hearts and minds,
Like noble works of art.

A reminder of laughter, tears,
And of a beating heart.

Then there's the one.
With whom I've grown,
A love that's blossomed,
Like a dandelion,
Through the ups and downs,
We've held on tight.
And now we stand here,
Challenging the distance if it ever keeps us apart.

In the Valley of Spring Lavenders

Can love withstand the trials of Time?
And in the void, a love sublime?
Only the brave, with hearts on fire,
Can conquer distance, and love's highest desire.

In the realms of thought where memories reside,
We humans cling to moments, side by side.

Like wisps of smoke, they gently play,
Drifting in and out, night and day.

Like a tapestry of moments, old and new,
a kaleidoscope of thoughts anew.

Whispers in the wind, they softly say,
'Remember me, in a fleeting way.'
And though they fade, like morning dew,
Their essence stays, in all we do.

In the Valley of Spring Lavenders

In separate ways, we had to sway
Different universities, we did choose
To grow and learn separately.

Challenges to test, Time to spend,
But we did face, with courage true,
And in our hearts, strength did grow.

Years passed by, and we did part,
But in our hearts, our love didn't fall apart.
A love that even Time could not unwind
A love that fate tried to bind.

Waiting to see your loved one is so hard,
Like trees waiting for spring's favourite bard.
Their branches bare, their limbs so still,
Longing for the warmth that will soon fill.

The wind whispers secrets in the trees,
Of love, that's strong, like winter's breeze,
That brings us strength, and hope, and light,
And fills our hearts with love,
Our forever guide.

You were worth all the miles in space,
All the moments lost in time and place.

I'd give up all the world's delight,
To hear your voice, my heart's only light.

In phone calls, we'd share our day,
If that means, I'd spend rest of my days,
Alone with hope,
The rest of our life is love-designed.

In the realms of the heart, where we reside,
A lover's trust is the key that distance cannot divide.

For in the depths of togetherness we share,
Patience is the anchor that our bond will repair.
Through life's ups and downs, through joys and fears,
Our trust is the anchor that wipes away our tears.

IBADAT

When years in love are spent together,
The heart loves something, the eyes see it clear,
A paradise sent from above, so dear.

The almighty's hand, a plan so grand,
A love that grows with each day so strong,
Together they stand, hand in hand.

In days of yore, we'd often meet,
For breakfasts and coffee, trips to mountains, nature's children,
In awe and wonder,
We were always full of praise.

But in six years, something changed.
The future, a winter haze of doubt,
Society's chains, our hearts bound.
The world, a complex, winding path,
Our dreams, a fleeting, fading wrath.

Yet still, we cling to our heart's desire,
Leaving our fortune for the Lord,
For us, we knew deep within,
Our meeting was what the entire universe conspired with.

In the Valley of Spring Lavenders

A time of eternity with you, was until now just a dream,
When did you land in my prayers?

In the realm of the unknown, where shadows play,
In silent whispers, your name I'd often say,
As midnight's silence banished all fear.

A time of eternity with you, until now a dream,
Tell me, when did you land in my prayers?

In twilight's hushed embrace,
We find our heart's refuge.

In your eyes,
My heart in flames,
Our souls entwined,
Like the stars in the midnight sky.
What are these big and small barriers,
When all we want is to fly?

While on a trip to the mountains,
Sipping our wines,
I asked you with a heavy heart,
'If we cannot make it to the end, will this love drift apart?'

Tears rolled down your eyes, and you proclaimed,
'How do I tell you the battle I am fighting,
The thought of being away from you, rips my heart.
I will do anything to make you mine,
Go to the stars or plead for you in all the shrines,
In every second, I should share with you,
The moments are fleeting, as they pass anew.
Whatever joys or sorrows come my way,
I should face them with you, come what may.'

JUNOON

Life is not always a fairytale,
A tale of wonder, a dream so grand.
It takes twists and turns without any clue,
And never warns of the trials anew.

One day you soar high on cloud nine,
Next, you plummet down the line.
The winds of change can bring such strife,
And leave you reeling, lost in life.

Such twists and turns came to us too,
We were full of joy and laughter,
Life's sweet sting.

Our smiles, like sunbeams,
As lovers, who tied the sacred knot.

Until one night,
The demon who hates love, peeped in.
Like a dark shadow on the wall and
A shard of glass,
Hope fell from the top of the hill,
Brutally crushed our love's thrill.

I landed in this world on a gibbous,
You came on a crescent,
Just like in the South, we came clashing.

Nothing in me was mine anymore.
What we feared took a flight,
Leading us to a crossroad.

My heart—ashes.
Once aflame with love,
Now reduced to embers cold.

Parched earth praying for the taste of rain,
The one who was my root of solace,
Now a heart's pain.

In the Valley of Spring Lavenders

In memories, I often find myself astray
Thinking about the last time we hugged in May.
How did you always know just when to stay?
Close to me, and pull me in, come whatever in our pathway?

But this time, it was different,
I couldn't hold you back,
And show you I care less.

This time,
I was tired of the mess
With no hopes of forever,
And no love to caress.

A prison of promises that I couldn't escape
The memories of laughter and tears we'd shared,
Were tainted by the pain, and the love that became unfair.

We became the cause of pain,
A love that turned to bitter strain,
The opposites wreaked havoc on their reign.

Our hearts, which once were not two, but one.

Who in the world would dare imagine,
That we would separate, and never renew.

The love we had, and which once shone through.
We were the flames that once burned bright,
Now reduced to ashes, without a light.
Our love, a memory, a distant past,
A chapter closed, forever to last.

But still, we hold on to what we had,
A love that was true, and the love that was mad,
For, in the end, it wasn't the end.

   In the Valley of Spring Lavenders

The bruises on the skin healed with time,
But the scars on our hearts lingered, like a crime.

For it wasn't the physical pain that cut so deep,
But the emotional scar, that we couldn't keep.

The memories of laughter sailed a different stream.
The tears we shed left their stains, it seemed.
Wounds of our hearts left a painful scream.

If at all you could see,
Drifting apart from you was a nightmare,
With no words to say.

I wish my tears could speak,
How painful it is to let a beat of my heart go,
How painful it is to see our land turn barren,
Where once the seeds of dreams were sown.

I recognized the two shades of love, the two sides,
In Good Morning kisses and shy smiles,
Like disappearing butterflies in the meadows.

We laugh for no reason,
And love in all seasons.

And then there's another side.
With the beauty, there's a helpless beast within,
A fierce and wild thing rages on.

With power that's hard to tame,
It longs for freedom and release from the chains,
But the heart, a fragile and delicate thing,
Tries to keep it caged, to keep it from harm.

It's a kind that we'd find at midnight.
With tears and pain,
life becomes dark like a vulnerable rain,
The world outside is waiting for us,
But there is a decision to make.

And so, the battle rages on,
A war between heart and mind,
But in the end, it is the heart that wins,
For love and beauty, they're not so tame.

But in the darkness, there's a glimmer of hope,
A light that shines like a beam of gold,
For in the heart, there's fire that burns bright,
A flame that flickers with gentle light.

In the Valley of Spring Lavenders

My cellphone rang at midnight,
I woke up in panic.

Listening to your voice, a sigh of relief,
You said,
'I am sorry for the pain I've caused by letting you go,
I never wanted anything, except you,
My mind always thinks of you, and I pray daily,
For you to forgive me and together we'd heal,
My heart still aches with every passing day,
For the love we had, cannot be replaced,
I am left with memories and a heart of stone.
I know our love wasn't for nothing,
And hope you will also believe,
I will be forever grateful for all that you've taught,
For me, there's nothing greater than your love for me,
Give us one more chance,
This separation has caused me unbearable pain.'

All the while, the clock was ticking,
Talking our hearts out, shredded in pain,
In the silence of the night, we'd confide,
Our deepest fears, our darkest tides.

We knew separation wasn't ours to gain.
With each passing moment, love will always unite.

In the Valley of Spring Lavenders

In twisted fate, we found our stand.
But who would have known
that destiny had a different plan?

What we had thought of doing was twisted once again,
Life again took an ugly turn,
And deviated from its plan.

A moment's pause, and it would all stall.
Who had imagined this to be our last call?

In life's early stages,
I was lost in time, too late,
I'd often find myself in rhyme, too early in my prime.

Maybe I had a vision, so blur,
Too late to change the course of my life's design.

Maybe I should've taken a different path,
Too early to realize my heart's true pursuit.

It is now too late to turn back,
And flip the pages of the book of fate.

MAUT

In the depths of my heart,
A burden I bear.

My life,
A tale not so fair.

Once a story of love,
Now a tale of woe.

6 April, 4:00 a.m.

My phone rings.
Restless I am,
The fearful voice says, 'He is gone ahead of our way...'

Silence numbs my heart and soul.

Grieving and screaming voices,
A deep shooting pain,
Breathless, I choke,
Body shivers from head to toe.

In the depths of my soul,
A cave so dark and deep,
I scream and wail,
A desperate shriek.

The leashes of silence, they strangle and bind,
My heart burns, ashes left behind.

The echoes of my cries linger and fade,
A haunting reminder of the pain I've caused.
The darkness closing in, a suffocating shade,
I'm trapped in a cave, with no escape in sight.

You promised me you would stay.
But Death came,
And took you far, far away.

You—the light of my life, gone too soon!
I am now lost in the darkest night.

I weep for the loss.
The pain so unbearable.

There was no goodbye, no parting word!
The absence of you—so sudden, brutal, and abrupt,
Heavier than any other burden that I can ever bear.

I can't mend what's broken and shredded.
All our dreams once knitted, now old yet incomplete.

The thread of hope, once so bright and bold,
Now hangs in tatters, a lifelong stain to hold.

Time, they say, heals all wounds,
But these scars run too deep.

The hurt, the pain, the shattered trust,
Leaving lifelong stains, permanent and deep,
I cannot recall the laughter; how did it sound?
When once it rang the doorbells of our house,
Silence is the demon with whom now I live,
The goodness of the world is gone now.

In the Valley of Spring Lavenders

What do I do with these ashes of desire,
Even the rivers have now dried up, with the scars.
I am left tangled, everything is dark,
The light of my life is dim.

The lantern retains the memories of You.

Losing you is heavy,
Tears streaming down my face, a river of pain,
As I cried and begged,
My voice in vain,
Insisted Lord, to take me along the way.

Death's icy grip, it did not wait,
Until I was ready, it did not hesitate.

In the whispers of the wind, I hear the past,
A chorus, a symphony that will forever last.

Our laughter, tears, and memories so clear,
Are the echoes that we hold so dear?
But now, in silence, I am left to face.

The emptiness that takes its place.
Your voice that once sang with joy and cheer,
Now but a distant memory, a fleeting fear.

Everything that was once mine, now lost to Time,
And only echoes remain, a haunting rhyme.

Without you,
Without your light,
My path is gray,
In the haze,
I will fade away.

The experts say,
'This world will end in a brutal way.'
But none of them will hear my plea,
My world ends for me every night,
And yet is born again the next day.

There's nothing that I can do,
Just trapped in this vicious loop.

In the depths of my heart,
A sorrow does dwell,
But if you were to seep into the truth,
It breaks my heart still.

Each day, I live in a world so cold,
Where the one I loved is no longer to hold.
You are in the cosmos,
So away, oh so bold,
Leaving me with a heart so cold,
I search for answers, day and night.

But the truth is, you're no longer in sight.
Your memory lingers, a distant light.
The pain of losing you,
A burden I carry, night and day,
A weight that I can't cast away.

I knew life was an art,
but pretending to be normal without you.
With each night my pillows are tear stained,
Swollen are the eyes.
Smiling now, I try to master the game.
Like a dart's aim.

                    In the Valley of Spring Lavenders

You were my light that shone so bright.
Without you, my world, a dark and endless night.
My life is now a canvas, empty and white.

In your eyes, my reflection,
I saw a shadow of me, once free and wild.

Now, a broken mirror, shattered and torn,
Without you, my pieces, no longer whole, nor born.
Tell me, without you, how to fulfill,
My soul's desire, my heart's will,
How to heal, how to mend,
My broken life, a shattered end.

In your embrace, my hope resides,
Without you, my dreams, they whine,
You were a promise of my poem,
but now this is all a rhyme.

Grief hasn't been empty.
It is so full and heavy.
Your absence from this realm, none can fill.
This emptiness is palpable.
The silent screams,
The echoes cry,
A lonely grief, refusing to die,
The heaviness that drowns, so hard to pull.

It was the rain that brought us joy by the day,
That has now taken my ship away.
And with it, our dreams, our hopes, our endless trip.
The waves that once caressed, now crash and roar,
As I'm left to mourn,
On a desolate shore.

In the Valley of Spring Lavenders

I count each night on every star.
You are somewhere, so far.

I fill the sky with poems of me and you.
For once, if my words traveled to you like a shooting star.
I miss you; I miss you,
Doing this alone was never our dream.

How could you just go, with the wind and the snow?
Didn't you remember the dream we dreamt long ago?
There was a castle we had to build,
with towers high and bright.
You said we'd work together, side by side, not as two,
but as one.

But now you're gone, and the castle's left undone.
The stones lie scattered, the walls crumble and fall.
And I'm left here, wondering why you left us all.

I thought we had something, something that would last.
But now you're gone, and our dreams are forever past.
The castle remains, but it's empty and gray,
A reminder of what could have been, if only you'd stayed.

In the Valley of Spring Lavenders

A dream of life again

In the valleys of our youth,
Where learning was the truth,
We laid the foundation of our days,
In classrooms, where love bloomed,
The lush green surroundings,
A haven for our minds,
Where we dreamt of our future,
Leaving our footprints behind,
The memories we made,
A treasure to hold,
Of the place where we began,
Our stories are to be told.

He says, 'My love, we will trace our strange journey from
the beginning,
And find the love that we have within.
We will laugh and love and live once more.
And our love will be forever in store.
We will cherish each moment, so dear.
And the day you're with me here,
We will both look back again, far and forever.
I will hold you, and we shall begin our life, all new,
You will see stars, galaxies and the cosmos celebrating,
We will both end and then begin again.
Please don't mourn anymore.
This isn't the end, because we shall meet again.'

In the silence,
We hear the echoes still,
Of our whispers,
And of the love that we fulfilled.

Though time may have passed,
And we've grown apart
The memory of young love,
Remains deep in my heart.

Months passed by, shattered and broken.
At midnight,
You appeared in my dream again,
In our garden, our home, which kept us sane,
With rainbows and flowers,
Tall trees with leaves,
Meadows and waterfalls,
And the sun's golden hue.

A soothing hug and I could finally breathe.
You came back and said, 'I am not really gone.
Go to a shrine in the Himalayas.
I will be there next to you,
You shall keep seeing me again and again.'

A dream so vivid and clear,
I know it wasn't just any other dream for sure.
A prayer answered.
I know you are finally here.

In the Valley of Spring Lavenders

For you, my love,
I've crossed the border so bold.
Through fields of light and oceans blue,
I shall travel across the shores,
In the realm of dreams,
Where fantasies are made.
I shall dance with fairies and
Soar high above the clouds.
With you by my side, my love,
I know that I can conquer the skies.

Bags packed, ready to go,
To seek answers, with hope in my heart,
I set my sight at the holy Kedar Nath in the Himalayas,
Where souls travel like ancient rivers and mountains,
And stand vigil as the timeless guardians of faith.

On the path uphill,
Bumpy patches lay in wait, a challenge to meet,
Sleet and rain, yet I stood my ground.
I fell
Yet rose again.
For in my heart I knew,
You were waiting for me to unravel the truth.

Up and up, miles to go.
Clueless about what was to come.
I still held on to hope.

Tired and exhausted from the walk,
I stopped next to a rock,
A small tea shop and local trail showing the way,
I sat there for a while looking at the snow-laden peaks.

Stood in front of me a stranger, a holy man,
In a saffron robe,
Giving me a hiking stick, said he:
'The temple is still far away.'

And in the blink of an eye, before I could understand,
He moved ahead quickly with a voice clear and loud,
'You may have lost him, but you're not alone.
His energies are entwined with yours,
He is now
Home within.
His love embedded in you,
The love you have is a deeper connection of the souls,
Always around you, in all things, big and small,
Everything is as it was, talk as much as you can,
He has just traveled to another home.'

In the Valley of Spring Lavenders

The message so clear,
You are indeed here.
The presence of the guide,
Attempting to help me along the way,
Keeps me buoyant still.

I felt love and divine at the same time.
Love—the shadow of the soul.
Love—devotion to God.
Love—the purpose of life.
An ineffable essence.

You came back to me, here again.
In your eyes, my heart's refrain.
In all our favorite songs, echoing memories,
Our love will play a harmonious dance,
Every single day,
And day after day.

The feathers rustling, whispers low.
In the breeze, our secrets and dreams.
In all the sunsets, blazing, golden bright,
A canvas painted, our love in sight.

In Sunday rain, we'll roam,
Hand in hand, the love which is home.
The drops on the pavement, a rhythmic beat,
A melody only our love can repeat.

You came back to me, here again.
With every breath, our love to sustain.
In every moment, our hearts are entwined,
Together forever, our love aligned.

You've come back to me, here again.
Reminders of our love, without any fail.

Our story isn't over.
We're lost and found.
Our souls intertwined,
We will see the sun again.
And we will see each other again.

You became my moon, my sun, my star, and my guiding
light.

My constant in the dark of night,
I pray to see you every morning and evening.

In your gentle beam, I find my way,
Through life's uncertainties, day by day.

Like a sailor charting a course by the sea,
I navigate life's waves, with you as my key.
You became my moon, my guiding light,
And my infinity!

Recently, a friend asked me,
'What happened to the person you've loved the most?'

And I was out of words,
Just tears, smiles and in my mind,
Our memories that linger the most.

How do I tell the world?
That I am still in love with You.

I made a promise
That you will be my life's poem.
When this life ends,
We will be back together again in our next.

We will sing and dance in the rain,
Go on walks in the night,
We shall do everything all over again.

Until then, wait for me there.
We will mend all our mistakes.

No matter what, under all circumstances,
This is our love, our only home.
It's just a matter of time.
Because the cords of our souls converge,
And become one,
Like infinity.

In the Valley of Spring Lavenders

Love Transcends

In a world of change, where time rewinds,
Love truly never ends.
It only transcends.
It is the essence of all the creeds,
We evolve and grow in our hearts and minds.

All human emotions go by,
As only love is free to fly.
It is the force that makes us sigh,
And fills our lives with light.
In this world of constant flux,
Love is the one thing that's brave and tough.
It endures through every test,
And always finds its way back to its nest.

There are no coincidences in love.
Destiny dictates meeting of people,
Only love is beyond life and death,
Beyond time and space,
From heaven we transpire,
Back to heaven we rise,
The seasons pass, the years go by,
Memories linger in the sky.
The lives we share never fade,

Somya Sharma

Love's embrace, a timeless shade.
For each time we arrive,
When lessons learnt,
We come back again for another one.

In the vastness of the universe, love does reign,
A force so powerful, it will never wane,
Through the eons of time, it sustains,
It's true, it never stains.
Forever alive, happy and free.
For it never ends.
It only transcends.

In the Valley of Spring Lavenders

In another life, in a happier place,
We'll meet again.
I will come to you with a smile on my face.

Crossing the stairway of heaven,
In the eternal spring,
As the angels dance and sing,
Celebrating our love again,
A gentle breeze will blow past us,
And hold us in a motherly embrace.

In daylight's soft, sweet glow.
In valley of spring lavenders,
Bright and serene,
Our love will be a melodious song,
Butterflies will play,
We'll dance an eternal dance,
We'll sing an eternal song,
Our souls united, at last.

We'll shine bright,
Upon the petals of the white light,
My heart knows we'll meet again,

In the eternal spring,
I will come to you with a smile on my face.
Until then, wait for me to hold your hand.

We shall meet again
In the valley of spring lavenders.

…

In the Valley of Spring Lavenders

Gratitude

My family—Kalpana Sharma (mother), Sanjay Sharma (father), Priyanka Sharma (sister) and Master Pixel—for their constant love and support and for standing by me, always.

Siddhartha Gigoo, for inspiring me.

Kanika Batra, for the cover art and design. Reachable @ kanika_artsyvision

Friends, relatives, colleagues, strangers and readers, for the blessings!

Notion Press, for publishing the book.